The Frog in Boys' Clothing

Roger L. Fields

Illustrations by Jaedyn Corbin

© 2023 Roger L. Fields

All rights reserved.

No part of this book may be reproduced, stored in a retrieval system, or transmitted by any means, electronic, mechanical, photocopying, recording, or otherwise, without written permission from the author.

ISBN (Paperback): 979-8-9894070-3-3
ISBN (Hardcover): 979-8-9894070-4-0
ISBN (eBook): 979-8-9894070-2-6

This book is dedicated to my grandsons, Cash and Cyrus.

The Frog in Boys' Clothing

When I was just a little boy,
oh, I'd say about your size,
I was walking by a narrow brook,
and much to my surprise,

On the bank just ahead, what did I see?
Sitting on the bank, on a big gray rock,
was a little frog looking back at me.

I wanted to hold the frog in my hand,
so I picked him up, you see.

He jumped from my hand, and where did he land?
Down my shirt, oh my, oh me.

I yanked off my shirt as quick as I could and tossed it on the ground.

With a ribbit-ribbit and a croak-croak, my shirt started to jump around.

My shirt jumped, and across the brook it went.
I chased as fast as I could go.

My shirt was gone. It was out of sight.
Where it went, I did not know.

Through the years, the little frog grew…

and grew...

AND GREW!
Being a good little frog, he took care of the shirt, and it still looks as good as new.

People say that boys and girls
walking by the brook
still see him swimming proudly
in my shirt the little frog took.

One of these days,
I am going back to the brook

and catch the frog in his nap,

**and upon the rock where he sleeps,
I will leave my favorite baseball cap.**

www.ingramcontent.com/pod-product-compliance
Lightning Source LLC
LaVergne TN
LVHW070536070526
838199LV00075B/6795

In his story, Roger Fields, captures the heart of generosity in a creative way that inspires readers to live their lives with open hands toward others.

Addie Jarrett, author of "Created to Shine"

Roger L. Fields was raised on a small farm in Northeast Oklahoma. Many hours of his childhood were spent sitting at an outdoor table listening to his Cherokee grandfather share stories from his own childhood. Those stories and their subtle messages had a profound impact on Roger's life. This book is the author's way of entertaining and passing on an innocent story to his grandsons, hoping the simple message will bring similar meaning to their lives.